EMOTIONAL ROLLERCOASTER

A Collection of Poems

D.A. Hopkins

Copyright © 2017. All rights reserved.

No part of this publication may be reproduced, stored in a retrieval system or transmitted in any way by any means, electronic, mechanical, photocopy, recording or otherwise, without the prior permission of the author except as provided by USA copyright law.

The opinions expressed by the author are not necessarily those of Revival Waves of Glory Books & Publishing.

Published by Revival Waves of Glory Books & Publishing

PO Box 596 | Litchfield, Illinois 62056 USA

www.revivalwavesofgloryministries.com

Revival Waves of Glory Books & Publishing is committed to excellence in the publishing industry.

Book design Copyright © 2017 by Revival Waves of Glory Books & Publishing. All rights reserved.

Photography taken by Payteena Treloar

Published in the United States of America

Paperback: 978-1-68411-181-7

Acknowledgments

I would like to acknowledge John Ginesi for the help in growing my writing skills and for the belief you had in me from the beginning.

I would also like to acknowledge Damion Thomas for the editing assistance.

Cover photograph by Payteena Treloar

Dedications

Damion, Emily, Hannabelle, Payteena, Kayne, and Dakodah

And a special dedication to my husband Lance Hopkins.

Who Am I By Name Alone

I am God's child first and forever

I am known by many different titles a daughter

I am a wife

I am a mother

I am a grandmother

I am a poet

I am by several ways known as a sister

I am an acquaintance

I am a loyal friend

I am a stranger

I am a cousin

I am an Auntie

I am a niece

But who is this person, they all call "Denise?"

She is a child to God

She is a niece

She is a cousin

She is a stranger

D. A. Hopkins

She is a loyal friend

She is an acquaintance

She is known to many a sister

She is a poet

She is a grandmother

She is a mother

She is a wife

SHE IS DENISE

Mothers Loss

Lost and alone

she doesn't know where too go

This mother is now stuck

she weighs up her options

And see's she is fighting against all the gossips

she stops and takes a look at this world

What have they done, to this lovable little girl

as she open's her eye's

she is faced with all their lie's

feeling alone and tired

She walks on to find

she is saying good-bye

Taking one last look around

before she lays down on the ground

As her eye's begin to silently close

she whispers her final prayer to die

Still she walks on, lost and alone

but the difference is now quite clear

For you can see her soul, has completely disappeared

D. A. Hopkins

A Bloody Rose

Roses here, roses there
Bloody roses everywhere

February brings them into our life
While others hide a broken wife

Young girls dream of their shining white knight
Well when do you think they will see it's nowhere in sight

Single men try everything to be romantic
If you ask every young girl, they still haven't learnt it

While romance will fill their heads
I'm still aware of the last lives it brought to death

The rose is not a passionate flower
But the very thing that causes humans lives to go sour

Nine months later in the mid of November
Young girls begin a day they will always remember

Emotional Rollercoaster

With a new babies cry with its first breath of life
There's a dad trying to work out how to tell his wife

A family is born, and a family is broken
This is all because of that bloody rose.

D. A. Hopkins

Christmas Dreams

I can't understand how one family can be dealt with so much
While others live their whole lives without so much as a touch
Well they always say karma comes to those who wait
Well I must say my patience is well passed its due date
Prayers are flowing constantly within this family
We might have to struggle, but we can always sing merrily
So many families in hardship and ruin, beaten down with unending pain
Longing for that special day, when peace can fill their hearts and lives again
so on a whimpering kiss, I send a prayer for everyone's blessings
Bring to us these lives that we have all well earned
And move along to those who have not yet learned
Joy, peace and loving times is what I see up ahead
These are just the prayers for my family that I've said
For it is now the time for our new lives to be unveiled and begin
Welcoming ends are heard off in the distance as people begin to sing
This is his birth month, the one true time for miracles
So sing praises with your favourite hymn

Emotional Rollercoaster

look over the horizon, watch as they all sing for him

For his love will wash away their dirty, secret little sins

So that January can deliver them their happier cleaner little lives

While I am left waiting, hoping for the prayer that it will one day be mine

A life where I can smile without regret or hesitation

In a future where this family can enjoy a simple celebration

This dream I hold very close for no one else to see

For if I shall die waiting for my dream, it will only destroy me

Along with everything I have ever truly believed

What this world means can become a very valuable cost

as my family continues to pray, for I have been all but lost

watching from heaven above, giving them everything

that I am able to carry upon my angle wings

D. A. Hopkins

A Childs Minute

Time for a nap

Said the cat

Time to play

Said the puppy, his tail waved

Time for class

Did you hear the bell, teacher asked?

Time for tea, called mum

Why you're always last young son!

Time for bed, dad called

Everything went quiet down the hall

Brush your teeth, yelled mum

Finally, all tucked in tight

They all dreamt peacefully, till morning light

Book Of Colour, My Daughters Poem

Imagine your life as a colouring in book

Inside this magical book

You can follow your own journey

to discover your true destiny Using your lovely pencils

You can join yourself on each page

As you set out to explore the world

and find out how much adventure

there is Outside of your tower

So bring a little bit of colour to your new world

Include the friends and family

To enjoy the adventure on this page mystical ride

to a place where dreams are made

D. A. Hopkins

Emotional Rollercoaster

This quotation poem was written by my daughter Payteena Treloar

This is her first step into the world of words and how deep they can be.

D. A. Hopkins

Dakodah

D is for all your "delightful smiles

A is for that all or nothing attitude

K is for the overwhelming kindness shown within your eyes

O is for the overwhelming loving feeling you give

D is for all the Dora you watch, continuously

A is for your abundance of energy you always have

H is for the millions of hearts you are going to be breaking

"Mummy's Thoughts"

So tiny and cute

With a personality to boot

So loving and caring

Your love is almost, overbearing

with love

Mum

D. A. Hopkins

Kayne

K is for the abundance of kisses we share

A is for your real little boyish attitude

Y is for all the yummy food you make and eat

N is for the never ending love we will forever share

E is for the endless laughter we share together

"Mummy's Thoughts"

So charming and boyish
Not knowing how precious
Overwhelming and bright
our happiness is my only light

with love
Mum

D. A. Hopkins

Hannabelle

H is for the many hearts you will break

A is for the appreciation you feel for love

N is for the never endless laughs we will have

N is for the loving nature that radiates from you

A is for all the happiness you bring into my life

B is for your bubbly smiles

E is for our endless memories

L is for all the love you give

L is for a lifetime we have together

E is for the eternal freedom I give to you

"Mummy's Thought's"

So bubbly and bright

You always have to be right

Compassionate and sweet

To everyone you meet

But never comparing

To the mum, you are forever sharing

with love

mum

D. A. Hopkins

Emily-Jo

E is for the emotions you show

M is for my little mother Hubbard

I is for your impatience

L is for all the love you send my way

Y is for your way or no way

J is for all the joy you are bringing my life

O is for the overwhelming passion you share

Emotional Rollercoaster

"Mummy's thought's"

So placid and true

Sent with eyes of heavenly blue

Filled with so much luck

For your always running a total muck

with love

mum

D. A. Hopkins

Payteena

P is for your petite little smile

A is for your bright angel eyes

Y is for all the yarns you tell

T is for the little temper you have

E is for the eternal happiness you bring

E is for the endless laughter that follows

N is for the nagging questions you ask

A is for your lady muck attitude

"Mummy's Thoughts"

You are my petite little angle eyes

With a story behind every lie

Giving attitude to everyone

Except the one you lovingly call mum

with love

mum

D. A. Hopkins

Damion

D is for the delightful child you are

A is for the angels that light up your way

M is for the manner you hold inside

I is for the independent gentleman I've raised

O is for the overwhelming warmth you bring me

N is for the loving nature within your heart

"Mummy's thought's"

So delicate and precious

Touching my palms so sensuous

All you need to remember

Is mummy will be here, for ever and ever

with love

mum

D. A. Hopkins

In Memory Of My Father

So long I needed to visit
But my heart didn't listen
Letting you know how much I love you so
Is now something you will never know?

Now that you are gone
I know I waited too long
If I could just have that one more chance
I would never treat it as just a simple glance

Now you have become my biggest memory
For you have gone to a place I cannot see
Knowing that we will never again kiss or touch
Makes me miss you so very much

My children are to young
To wonder why pop hasn't rung
My heat is now empty
For you, it always had plenty

Emotional Rollercoaster

I really do need you back
You were the only one, who had my back
For I know deep down inside
You loved me more than words could describe

For it is only now that I realise why you didn't want me around
You knew it would be too painful to watch you drown
But as long as I am still alive
You too will continue to survive
For I will always be your darling little Denise
Who hopes you will forever rest in peace

ALLAN THOMAS HOLMES
1ST JUNE 1954-22ND OCTOBER 1997

D. A. Hopkins

Scream

I want to scream
Please someone help me
But what good would it be
No one will hear me

Poverty Defines True Wealth

I don't know if human's will ever see

every soul born, is right where it's meant to be

For the rich to become the richest

there has to be a place for the poorest

The entire world is built up from the same level of dirt

each soul is born without knowledge to cause hurt

Humanity teaches us what a human's life is worth, by money and glory

I am to believe all lives are priceless, every soul fit's to tell Earth's story

The luckiest to be born, is that of a poor man

he learns the treasures, of everything he can

D. A. Hopkins

Those born into all riches have no true understanding of richness

seeing us not as human's, but those living in poverty as an illness

Love starts from the soul, and from there it is taught to grow

the rich find another kind of love, one only brought with dough

Love, trust, compassion and grace, defining the difference in richness and wealth

t'is the beggar off the street who climbs the toughest road to earn his wealth

He is the most blessed man, he is rewarded with the most valuable key

for his wealth is humanly uncountable

for only God knows, the true value of he..

Emotional Rollercoaster

A Birthday Kiss

As I woke up this morning
I instantly began mourning
For I should be holding you, this special day
but I know that there is no possible way
Wondering if you'd think that I would forget
is just one more thing I am left to regret
I pray that we will be re-united together again soon
till then I've blown you a birthday kiss, I sent via the moon
Overwhelmed, I feel as if I love you even more today
today is special after all, it is your birthday
But I couldn't forget you no ifs, buts or maybes
for you were blessed forever to be my baby
You are now my six-year-old lovable Hannabelle
And no one on Earth could ever love you as well
Known now and forever as a very special day
for it was on this day, that you became my daughter in every way

D. A. Hopkins

A Tear For Daddy

Even after sixteen years
still I cry your daughterly tears
Every year upon this day
will always only now be known
as the date that God took my loving dad

1st June 1954- 22nd Oct 1997
Allan Thomas Holmes

LOST LOVE "In Aussie Slang"

I was in love with the most lovable sheila
but she did darn take off with me heeler
Overnight, she had packed their bags
not just me dog, gone too with me scallywags
Left with just a simple note
she had found a more loving bloke
Heartbroken to have lost them all
I gave me mate Bluey a call
Together we drank more than just a slab
ending up so hammered, he had to call us a cab
As the lonely days passed and tears filled me eyes
by crikey it hit me, suddenly I came to realise
What a bloomin idiot, she deserved such love and respect
every night boozin with me mates, my true love I did neglect
I'm gunna cut out me drinkin and win her heart back
fair dinkum fella's, you can flamin bet on that!

D. A. Hopkins

DAMAGED MY TRUE LOVE

When it comes to love, I AM poisonous
don't let me curse another, leave me loveless
For the first time in my life, I felt your pain and cried for your heart
my heart finally hurts knowing I passed on this pain from the start
Please find help to set your heart free
trust me, it's not a life you recover from easily
Damaged goods I told you I was unrepairable
but somehow you managed the impossible
Unlovable for my entire life
yet you had no problem, getting me to become your wife
Yes, it's been more than both of us should have ever had to bear
But at this moment every cell in my body is overwhelmed
so I really do care
Please don't enter my world of pain and despair
you don't deserve it here
you are so kind and patient
and your heart is filled with such love

Emotional Rollercoaster

I'm sorry I let myself fall in love knowing it would poison you soul mates forever and eternity, my love belongs only to you...

D. A. Hopkins

Birth Cursed From

A lifetime of pain and suffering

winning me over, to be loved and trusted

Now I find I'm alone again

it always ends the very same

will my life ever be more than just pain and nothing to gained?

Emotionally damaged from the very start

setting me free from my head, as my body now packs up

sentencing me to this year confined to this bed

Finally, I've become drug free

Nexium and Valium will always stay with me

you have now become so stressed

it's leading your love to abandon me

I'm cursed, I have been since the day of my birth

destined for a lifetime of nothing, even dirt has more worth

Sorry I'm no good, I recall telling you this at the start

it's me this time, to be left with the broken heart

I treasure our year before, filled with pure love and safety

my heart and soul will now and forever ...will belong to you

matey

Wedding Band

This life is not as it should be
pick up your wife, can't you see
You're her husband, stand up!
give her a reason to again believe
She means everything still to this family
shutting the door, to leave her totally Alone
Do you actually know her at all?
damaging her heart and soul
from deep within, it's cold
Loneliness consumes her it's been so long
it must be asked...do you still love her?
Are you willing to help her to her feet again?
shall you just sit back and watch
as your love begins the journey towards end
This is completely left for only you to do
her husband to declare how much does she really mean to you
do you still really care?
Will you step up or let her rot?
into that web of depression
you see it very clear

D. A. Hopkins

Love and care

or fall into despair

will you help your wedding band?

Setting You Free

I am here today to set you free
but inside of me you shall always be
You will never truly leave
as your love and memories, continue to live on in me
I have come to terms with you leaving
your love shall forever continue as long as I believe
I will forever miss you very much
for I know it's impossible to again kiss or touch
Although you were never rich or royal
your heart remains eternally loyal
So these are the hardest words for a daughter to have to say
I pray you hear these words from my heart today
From your darling little Denise
saying my final good-bye to my dearest daddy
Praying you will forever, rest in peace

ALLAN HOLMES
1954-1997

D. A. Hopkins

Empowering Innocence

A single rose grows with purity within an in-fenced field
from that very moment it buds
watch as its passion and grace intertwine
It begins to bloom with such confidence
showing off its elegance with complete dominance
For you are left totally unaware of the entire field of daisies
swaying away
such passion and grace, still exists within the heart of humanity
Our worlds future completely relies on peace to become heard
but it depends on how far has man let it go
our hearts hold hope for the same entity
Peace, love and harmony for those who choose to believe
Jesus freed that curse we'd received by Adam and Eve
they have found love and peace Taking it upon themselves
they help the next man to be free within God's own time
and we will come to see heaven on earth
For it is still a gift we all receive
at the first hour of our birth

Addiction

I want you gone

so why are you still holding on

I don't need you anymore!

so let me go

go on, I've shown you the door

I've found my peace within the grace of God

his love is so much more, than you could even try to endure

My freedom is awaiting me please

I beg you to set me free

I DON'T WANT YOU ANYMORE

DO YOU NOT SEE?

I AM NO LONGER YOUR'S

being set free and redeemed by God

I have received a brand new set of eyes

D. A. Hopkins

A Need To Feel

The feeling is dwells from within
a desire to cut starts to begin
I reach out for an innocent blade
needing to feel something again
As the blade starts to penetrate my skin
I can feel the relief from deep within
I lie so peaceful, I long for this feeling to stay
Lost in this world unable to make another day
But the blood begins flowing to fast this time
Its release renders me powerless to fight
My body grows cold and dim
I penetrated a little too deep into my skin
Unable to move, I'm restricted to lie here to die
This body left lifeless, as my soul takes to the sky

Eternally Damned

I recall prayers from this bed
those left unsaid and those I truly meant, with every breath
as I continue to lay here, still in this bed
Not one of them ever answered
is there anyone else I could maybe, talk to instead?
My hopes along with all my dreams
forced to face the cruel truth, that these will never be
So why Do I continue to stay?
once again with my faith, the option is simple only pray
Not one friend listened to my cries
Lord come for me, take me away
I am only human and yes, I have made my mistakes
Nothing in this world could have proven, that I had told the truth
I obeyed every task you set, all of them proven impossible for any person
I'm weakened please I beg, no more
" I ask ye' oh Lord" have I not endured equal to that of my shame
forever to wander earth, lost and betrayed

D. A. Hopkins

will I ever again see mankind the same

Oh Lord desperate for guidance and reassurance

I'm at an all-time critical low

will I ever again trust humans working with me

as I creating a new home, no!

I did everything humanly possible to achieve your tasks

You are clearly delusional to all who I asked

now the answer's a little late

for all I can come to see

the only reasonable conclusion is

"I AM, ETERNALLY DAMNED"

Final Prayer

Alone again...

will this confusion ever end?

I have lost all of my hope

for I no longer know how to cope

What do I do

to get back the life I once knew

Confused and dazed

for I have lost the children I raised

I am praying with ALL I have left

help me get through the rest...

D. A. Hopkins

Hidden Tears

A whole year has past
how much longer will this really last
The harder she tries
the more her hope slowly dies
Why must this mother have to fight
just to hold you all so tight
Telling you how much she loves you
is something she REALLY needs to do
No one has listened to her cries
she's finding it harder just to get by
She smiles and laughs
to cover her broken and bleeding heart
No one can even tell
she has learnt to do it so well
She needs you all to know
she never wanted too go
She hopes and she prays
you will all forgive her someday....

Rotten Luck

Will I ever get off this blooming roundabout?
why must I always need to scream and shout
As things just start to settle
I will be forced to take on a new battle
Will it ever end
I need a really good friend
Someone that will listen
and not have to be my competition
Someone who cares
a friend is all I need
But enemies are all I ever see
will it ever stop
this lifetime of endless, rotten bad luck...

D. A. Hopkins

Choice Of Life

Recalling that day at school
When the teacher set out that task
what do you want to be? she asked the class
My answer was simple
so I had thought...
to be a mum, I'd have six kids and live on a farm
If you would believe, that's exactly what I received
but it was not made to come with ease
For the fathers I had sadly chose
became prideful and greedy!
never till now did it cross my mind
my babies would someday not need me
Leaving me again to think, what do I really want to be
as faith would have it already planned out, so I'd soon see
For the FIRST! time direction, would finally enter my life
poetry writer was soon to amount of me
after I'd become a wonderful wife
Now poems are continuously raging within my head
everything wanting to be read
as I failed English on an epic scale

Emotional Rollercoaster

it's hard to believe, this dream inside my head

At 38 years of age I see my life heading back to school

maybe this time around, I won't play the class fool!

D. A. Hopkins

The Question

If an Oyster can turn a grain of sand
into a beautiful creation, known as pearl...

Why is it us humans, can't seem to get it together
and change Our World, into something so much better...

Stuck

This future I cannot bare

so why do I still care

The torture still lives

but there's nothing left to forgive

The hurt, and the pain

now it all feels the same

My love for my kid's

is the only reason I still live?

This life I would love to end

for there is nothing else left to mend

Push me a little

I appear to be a little bit Stuck

Here in the middle

D. A. Hopkins

Visiting Our Land Downunder

The place downunder I'm happy to call my home
if you plan on a visit, here's somethings you do need to know
Kakadu, is a place you need to take the time to see
such magic you will never won't to leave
But if your arms outside of the boat...
It WILL end up down a crocodile's throat
Ayres rock, is a must place to have on your list
simply this you cannot afford to miss
As the sun descends over the land watch as it's colours change
you'll be mesmerised by pure bliss
Coober Pedy, for those slightly intrigued with the underground
for it is here, a quite little town where all their houses are found
Ballarat, is for those looking to pan for gold
And you can still today find a little gold
Well, that's what I've been told
I recommend you don't swim in the oceans at the top end
surrounded by oceans the rest, feel free to jump in
BUT if you happen to see a fin
I highly recommend that you start to swim

Emotional Rollercoaster

With nights call when offered pull up a chair grab a beer and
relax
there's just one small catch
Don't ever be the first to fall asleep
Aussie's find extensive pleasure in an innocent prank
Especially to those asleep
Enjoy your stay and from the Land downunder
we all say "G'day" and look forward to seeing you again
as we already know you had a great stay

D. A. Hopkins

Owed To Dolly

Raised in a world without any morals
Lead me to a lifetime of sorrows
Words that were written within Dolly's songs
was the only reason I even took this challenge on?
Refusing to have my children raised that very same way
I focused on this world that she always sung about
From singing Dolly's song's it would see me begin to pray
the crossing over into this world of happier day's
Was much harder than her song's did ever say
believing only in her words during the hardest of time's
I'd sing her songs till it would eventually calm my mind
but with Dolly as my guide I took it all in my stride
twenty-one years after I first stepped onto this hopeful walk
It is the one thing I did right, to seek out this world she spoke
unknowing it was her alone that filled me with strength and
hope
To leave the only world in which I'd known
And guide us to this little town, we now call home
So thank you Mrs Dolly Parton for letting your lyric's be known

Emotional Rollercoaster

they alone were the power in which I 'finally' found our loving

home

D. A. Hopkins

Fading Into The Dark Of Night

As my life slowly slips away
this time I WILL NOT PRAY
for he too hath left me this way
Month's tick by and not a soul stop's by
this moment in time I start to wonder why
During my darkness and addiction
love poured in from every direction
I lay here now as each day passes
memories of me here as I slowly perish into darkness
My heart and soul had become God's alone
even he has left me again unloved, abandon, worthless
Friend and family trust had them all torn away
my fellowship leads me to believe I had a say
None of them notice as to my dismay
I was right at the very start Trust in no one
giving peace back to my heart its only me who I can believe
Poetry takes my heart my mind and my soul
to world's you could never even dream
I will consume myself with fairy's and elves

Emotional Rollercoaster

forget the belief that anyone would've ever cared for me
    They all only ever cared for themselves
    And now they leave me here, completely alone

D. A. Hopkins

Life Goes On

The world is still turning

but my heart continues yearning

The sun is shining

but I am forever crying

The world is still giving

but I have stopped living

The pain is still there

but I no longer care

The tears have stopped flowing

the hurt and pain, continues growing

How much more can a mother take

before all she's forced to do is hate

Penance

her mind hypnotic

thoughts ticking around

good god I've got it

she jumps up off the ground

a plan indeed

but he puts up a fight

for he had possession of speed

a man dies through the night

he has his sentence

for throwing a knife

he now pay's his penance

behind bars for life

D. A. Hopkins

Goal

I need to find a goal

no longer to live life of a broken soul

Living a lie just to get by

I've past all the pain

And left with their stain

a new life is now in reach

This new world beside the beach

no longer do I continuously pray

Hidden for so long

I don't know where I belong

To start it all over

is harder than it is for an alcoholic to stay sober

Where do I begin?

how far do I jump in?

This new life is rather very frightening

I'm scared and taunted

But no longer am I haunted

the first steps I have begun taken

To walk with my head held high and awaken

I have finally found my soul

Emotional Rollercoaster

Now Lord, I ask what is to be my goal?

D. A. Hopkins

Begin To Boil, Technology

I'm about to blow my stack
another poem I'll never get back
CRASH....this time my phone lets me down
hours of typing lost, try to recall simple words
Technology is driving me insane
but there's the irony
the greatest poets and artists of our time
as in those better days
were declared mentally insane

It was intended for another poem to share
In that frustrating moment as I lost that poem
My rage delivered this work of art so instead, enjoy my love for technology

Time To Move

My faith is in you Lord
trapped to this bed I'm bored
How much longer shall I be still
for I know this is by your will
I'm alone and at your mercy
I've given up friends and family
My faith is struggling, oh Lord
I pray that you hear my call
I've been still by not a choice of mine
learning lessons through your will and time
Patience is growing to an all-time low
let's get this operation done come on let's go
I've learnt who I am, and I do pray
so let's get moving before I fade away
Give me strength to handle this operation that awaits
so that I may again see the sunlight on my face
For I feel it up over the horizon
this new year will bring a new life one

D. A. Hopkins

Mothers Day

What is Mother's Day
it has become meaningless to me
to have none of my children on this day
what more do I need to say
how heartless and cruel can they be
do they really know what they are doing to me?
to be hurting me so bad
it makes me even more mad
to use my children in their twisted game
just so they can get their own way
is there not any other way?
I hope and I pray
but it's been useless till this day
when will it be my place to have a say
with my words that flow of truth
When will have my babies back
I can gladly say that this is the day
you have finally all met your match
These children long for their mother
This family can never be forced apart by any other

Emotional Rollercoaster

this is their life of freedom that they finally found

forever this family will always be bound

D. A. Hopkins

Lance

I need your love, so much

I never dreamed this would come from your touch

my soul has grown into you

It's a love, I had never before knew

Your kind and so patient

For this I must proclaim

I took my sweet time

to see love myself in your perfect way

You love me for me

what more can I say

What you've always see in me

I can only say

by God's grace and your faith

Did we come to see the day

When I would finally say the words...

"I do"

Skies Full Of Wonders

See the sight of a full moon in the dark of night
if done just right, it's a magical sight
Watch as the sun descends off the edge of the earth
it's flame's extinguish as if by the ocean's thirst
Look deep into the sky at night
you'll be surprised by your delight
All of the heavens glory
will return again the very next morning
So send a wish upon your favourite star
you'll never guess that your wish could travel so far
So at the end of every busy daylight
breathe in the gift of heaven's blissful night
I guarantee, it'll help you sleep peaceful and right
well into his new mornings delight

D. A. Hopkins

Noah's Ark

As all the paired animals were boarded onto the Ark
Noah, with his final list ticked them off as a simple task
No one saw the two flies go pass
sneaking aboard under a golden mane, on a horse with class
While the flies were free to roam
Eventually they started their journey on home
When they finally got to the top of the Ark
looking for their home, but nothing could be seen in the dark
Since that day that they were stowaways
arrogantly believing humans stole them that day
And have vowed since that day they decided we were to blame
humans would have to pay
so they terrorise us even still to this day
The secret I've heard is they were never even invited onto the ark
all who were on the list voted if the flies be added to the task
Not to Noah's surprise for they were a pest and for the entire time
not one vote did they receive no, not from one single mind
They would never again return back to their homeland

Emotional Rollercoaster

to everyone's disappointed just think

wouldn't our summer's be grand

D. A. Hopkins

Undoing The Curse Of That First Sin

It started at the dawn of creation
to honour, love and protect every nation
it wouldn't take long, for humans to stray
for I'm to believe, it was that very same day
the father of all creation returned to earth
before he would set their punishment, he'd listen to their reason first
for the price of your sin, spoken with a disheartened breath
you and all your descendants, shall be punished by death
sin ravished the land
so the father had to come up with a plan
Noah he told, build an ark for your family and a pair of every creature
with not one question asked, he obeyed the word of his teacher
the towns people pointed and laughed
nothing would come between Noah and his ark
on completion to his task
all that were called, boarded onto the ark
those people that pointed and laughed

Emotional Rollercoaster

as the rain flooded the land, they wished back their harsh remarks
when God opened heavens gates all of the world was erased
now he did think, may I have been too harsh
with sin washed away
it would lead a new way
as they off loaded the ark
humans don't learn so well, God made a snide remark
as God would come to tell
sin again conquered the earth, but he promised no one else would be killed
years passed by, God knew the only way to clear Adam n Eve's curse
was to have the curse somehow reversed
so he sent his only son, born to a young virgin to become his mum
this child would have to live life pure and holy, for he was to carry the sins of man upon himself
and be lead to a brutal an inhumane death upon that cross
the cross where his pure blood spilled too free and redeem all of man's sin

D. A. Hopkins

he was to bless us even more, with the holy spirit to dwell

within

God knows this was the only way

Silence Bestills The Night

As the world shuts down
lavish ladies draw their gown
Rest comes while they comb their hair
while others are fighting the midnight air
All living the lives they had exactly detailed
not a thought goes out to the ones who failed
Homeless man, where was his fall?
Does anyone care, that no one heard his call
One moment a blink in time and it's lost
the next one to fall, that could be anyone's cost
The wise will gaze their eyes into the skies
for he is the only one you need to recognise..

D. A. Hopkins

God's Plan

Mid-summer rainfall
everything fades till you recall
innocence in the sound of an infant's cry
an old lady dies with an innocent good-bye
the glimpse of a magical rainbow
no matter how old, will make you feel whole
the whisper of a gentle breeze across the land
makes me realise how small I really am
A loving smile in a stranger's eye
could be the one that would later die
I hear heavens gates can open wide
for by the end of my life, I will have an army of loved ones by my side
destiny calls me to spread his love and grace
as I live a life beside God, with his love and mercy
all it ever really comes down to
Is love him the way that he loves you
Maybe give him a gentle curtsy, when he says "how do you do"

Faith

I lie here with all my memories
realising the full cost of this new life through it all my faith was
kept strong
I know now God knew it all along
The path had to be taken that very way
as I grow to know Jesus more every day
I realise God was always one foot ahead
That's the only reason I now lay here in this bed
Every bumpy path that I chose
all the prayers that were left unsaid
he knew the road I'd need
or I wouldn't have all my babies you see
now this new life I breathe
is getting to really know him and his journey
the bible I've had for so many years
now for the first time enters my ears
no longer just in faith
but in Jesus I will now forever praise

D. A. Hopkins

Storm Of Hope

As the storm rolls in
the lightning crashes and the thunder roars
so peaceful, so it would seem
as the water drips off the end of its leaves
the storm is just passing through
As it has nothing better to do
it fills an empty heart with hope
and takes away the pain of the broken
but the storm will come to an end
and the pain will again begin
As you wait longing once again
for the next storm to begin
for everyone's soul is wishing
There's hope for something at the end

Confusion

Too lonely, to be awake
but too scared to sleep
Too painful too live
but no way to die
To lost to keep going
but too stubborn to stop
To confused to know how
but smart enough to know why

D. A. Hopkins

A Mothers Cry

A mother's cry is never heard
but it can always be felt
A mother's tear is never felt
but it can always be seen
A mother's pain is never seen
but it has always been
She learnt about this cry
before her baby first caught her eye

Opened Eyes

It's time to turn this around
the answers I have finally found
The minute I looked into your eyes
I immediately remembered how to be alive

If I didn't go through all those years of pain
my life wouldn't be the same
Your birth nothing less than magical complete power of God's love

For you shone through complete demonic darkness
ever since I have been more than blessed
you re-opened my heart
So I could again play the part

I've been given a second chance
This time around, I won't forget to dance
to love open and freely
Its finally great to again be me

D. A. Hopkins

I've turned my frown upside down
And it's from God's gift when pure innocence was born
my sixth child, a blessed tiny little girl

Past Of Horror

I wake up with another tear

for I have again relived the nightmare

will it ever leave

when will I again be able to see

the past is forgiven

so why is it still living

my heart was broken

but soon after it was frozen

let it lye and the past die

for I have a life to give

but the past is still being relived

how do I stop this past of torcher so I can find my future?

D. A. Hopkins

Torn

I sent a prayer, from deep in my soul
it was answered, by our loving God
I was going to heal, my heart of sorrow
but, she's not coming tomorrow
Lies, lies, lies
I love you mum your actions, I do despise
Hope, joy and peace filled my heart
Hearing your voice say, you're coming to visit
Lies, lies, lies
Bouncing with such joy
Feeling like a small child
Finally receiving a new toy
Now tears feel my eyes
You lied, You lied, You lied

A Childs Plea

Dirty rotten scum

to take the life of an innocent one

taken my childhood

but not thrown into adulthood

you've given me a life of pain

certainly never again to be the same

but I've found freedom within Gods kingdom

where the past is a welcome singing

D. A. Hopkins

Why Am I Here

I love with my soul

but my soul is gone, so why do I love

My eyes are to see you's

but you's aren't to be seen, so why do I need my eyes

My fingers are to feel you's

but you's I cannot feel, so I have no need my fingers

My arms are full of cuddles

but there's no one to cuddle, so why do I have these arms

My legs are to lead you's the way

but I have no one to lead, so my legs have no use to me

My life is for only you's

so without you's, why do I need this life

Depression

I laugh when I'm not happy
I sleep when I'm not tired
I eat when I'm not hungry
I talk when there's no one to listen
I run when there's nowhere too go
I pray but is there anyone there
Emotionally I have had all I can take
my head hurts
my body aches
all because I made a mistake

D. A. Hopkins

Answers

I love you all with my whole entire heart
every second, I'm left to wonder why we're apart
I try to work out what I must've done wrong
how many mothers sing this sad song?
But there are no answers to my questions
Every year we have spent together
is now embedded in my heart forever
I think hard and long
does this pain really belong?
Still ...there are no answers to my questions
Strength I once had to carry on
is nearly dead and gone
I say a prayer every night
to give me strength to stay and fight
I still ask, "why us" were we on the wrong bus
I weep a tear with every second
how do I live like everyone reckons?
Still ...I get no answers to my questions
I stay here fighting for just one more touch
am I really asking way too much

Emotional Rollercoaster

I love my babies with every beat of my heart
please I beg you, stop keeping us apart
Still ...no answers to my questions
I'm only left to Guess
that God's reasons, are truly his very own

D. A. Hopkins

In Need Of Strength

Lord I cry out to you

In my weakness and shame

Cover me and support me as I need you

Give me strength for success to obey your truth

Guide me as I stray to fix my eyes upon you

Heal my hearts wounds and demons too

Let me live with peace again

In your everlasting defence

Forgive me of my guilt and shame

I need you in my life everyday

Forgive my reckless behaviours

I welcome you to be my saviour

I alone cannot restrain from my sinful way

Give me the strength to kneel and pray

Guide my heart to be true to everyone

I surrender to the Gods truly gracious love

A Mothers Wish

My babies, my angels, my hope
You's are all I will ever need to cope
From heaven you came
My life will never be the same
To feel each one of you grow
No one else will ever know
We have formed a bond that's so strong
It will last so long, even till after I'm gone
My life is dedicated to you
To teach and love
to look and learn
to speak and listen
to hope and pray
You's will be happy, every God given day

D. A. Hopkins

Give Peace A Chance

Our men and women sent off to war
how many will end a life before they're return
will they ever speak of what they saw?
sadly, we hear of another dead infant
why is there still so many that are killed?
are looking for something instead of the innocent
More homeless families forced out on the street
who will be the next family to admit defeat
The world is no longer a family place to dream
What have our lives now come to
If you are to save a stranger's life
You can guarantee that they'll sue
What is happening to our human race
This is where I ask the very truth from you
can you describe your next door neighbours face?

Awaiting

Roses are red,
violets are blue,
Jesus is in heaven,
is he waiting for you!

D. A. Hopkins

Baby

You were never seen by us, that privilege sadly was not for us
an extravagance we were overwhelmed by the thought of your embrace
The entire twelve weeks you were a joy to have known, even without being seen
hearing about your arrival was a blessing at the time you were conceived
For life hadn't been easy and we had all asked God, we even plead

We wait upon the day, you will finally meet us
having the honour to love and learn with you, sadly not for us
It breaks my heart as you part, you had already embedded love into my heart
Just knowing we will now, forever be kept apart

God has other plans for your love that's so strong, blessing us from the start
we continually pray, maybe he'll decide to let you stay around

Emotional Rollercoaster

but the intense pain of tears and loss, are constantly falling all around
just let it be known we all desperately wanted you to become part of us

We all will love you for eternity, you are now forever one of us, although it was only for a very slight second, it was better than never
You are from this day on, embedded into our hearts forever
the impact you have left unborn young one' 'my beloved grandchild

"Angel" 2012

D. A. Hopkins

This Is The World In Which We Live In

A young mother forced to sell her soul for apiece of gold
For the four babies starving at home all alone
No one cares about the way she wears her hair
They couldn't care less about the dress she wears.

A young boy walks a lonely street at night
Hunger burns his tiny tummy "it's not alright"
Climbing up into an old man's van
Making this where the end of his life just began.

How can we humans still live this way
Seeing a life in trouble and turning to walk away
If you live with more than others, you are the one full of share
For each human was born the very same.

There's a loving mama of twelve
She believes in a heaven and hell
An honest day's work is her only yield
Her hands now forever bleed from the cotton fields

Emotional Rollercoaster

A mother says goodbye to her only son
As an army man hands him his first shotgun
All he is told to survive is "be strong son
And do try to make it home to your mum."

What is this humanity meant to believe?
Why doing everything is not all this government has you'll need
Hide your beliefs from the streets
If you are seen passing by the people will now all scream you are a terrorist
Racism has gone far beyond the colour of our skins
Is this really the world you wish to live in?

D. A. Hopkins

Amnesia

I lay here in this bed
Listening to this story you's have all said
Not realising it was forgotten inside my head
And how we were all, almost dead.

How sad a story you are about to hear
But never fear love and happiness does persevere
The pain and amnesia have settled in here
As days and months pass my mind starts to clear.

Tragedy hits as I begin to understand
Hearing those words 'car crash' while you're holding my hand
Still worse to come, Teena's not good, I don't know where I am
Take me away, don't say anymore I can't understand

Amnesia is not as good as I once had planned
I wish I could remember
What went wrong to land our family this way
I wish I could remember
How I lost control and hurt us all so bad

Emotional Rollercoaster

I wish I could remember

I wish for a better day

I wish

I wish

I wish

How do you return back to life?

When everything you have to learn over

What a burden to you being your wife

Standing it hits me unable to walk I fall over

My baby on life support

I crumble as your mother

Bed to bed I reach for a touch

Painfully I have to leave, leaving you with no other

Amnesia resets my brain

And the next day we all go through it again

Pain ripples off my bed

Our family's hearts all currently dead.

D. A. Hopkins

Hearts Desire

Fears fade as I drift in your cloud,
Your touch healing all wounds.
Lost in your scent, my soul sings, embracing the joy of your love song
Growing further into you,
My mind turns to hearts desire,
Finally, my anxious soul rests.

This poem was written by Lance Hopkins
A poem written for myself to show me the way he feels about his wife

D. A. Hopkins

Whispers In The Night

As this world of ours closes down

somewhere there lays a lonely young girl

she whispers out to the goblins from another town

asking for the enchanted wall to be open to join their realm

filled with fairies and pixies and magic

her night is filled with delightful magical stories

where this young girl now starts to forget is tragic

back in this land her family is given such a fright

for they had awoken in the dark of the night

finding their beloved Jezzabelles bed empty

not one of them knew of this other realm

not even Moneque her twin sibling had been told

frantic as they walked the dark and cold streets

Emotional Rollercoaster

with no sign of the girl they all missed dearly

police and searchers went far and wide

but couldn't ponder where she would hide

for the fairies had begun to wash away her precious memories

they had been longing for her to join them for many of skies

as the sun arose with the morning light

Jezzabelle had forgotten her life

forever to live on within their realm of Picmindo

coming out only on the whispers of young lonely cries

Moneque would soon be next to discover their secret realm

soon to join her twin, during the dark cries of night

D. A. Hopkins

An Aussie Family Barbie

A celebration is about to take solitude here
Wonder what is in their thoughts as they draw near
Watching as families gather united with play
Happy as the different generations go about the day
Children giggle every little girl running to be found
While teenagers flop all over the ground
Grandparents sit back in their deck chairs
While mums and dads count off in pairs
Cousins reunite as if never parted
Where is auntie? It's sad she recently departed
Uncle cries all day long as if no one hears
Sizzles from the barbie signals food is near
Swarms of hands and arms try to fill up
Throw the slightest crumb up in the sky
Your day is now invaded the seagulls have arrived
Ending the busy day is a million kisses with nowhere to hide
Car doors slam and away they drive off into the night
The grounds are empty once again
I continue to sit here
They never even seen me in the end

Emotional Rollercoaster

How many lives do we simply pass?
Never to see the other human class

D. A. Hopkins

Lifes Blink

As he blinked his eye's
The year's passed him by
What happened, to my innocent life?

Lance

L is for your forever loyalty

A is for your new argumentative side

N is for the niggly things I ask of you

C is for the way you caution everything

E is for our eternal life too come

"wife's thoughts"

Clean your ears out
And I wouldn't need to shout
If you weren't always a grouch
I wouldn't have to scream and shout

Love Denise

D. A. Hopkins

Quotations

'Love is forever
So be found early'

'An empty broken heart
Is a dangerous weapon'

Notes

Notes

Notes

Notes

www.ingramcontent.com/pod-product-compliance
Lightning Source LLC
Chambersburg PA
CBHW070116080526
44586CB00013B/1309